This Book Belongs to

D' Angelo

A Gift from

Mary Moore

On the Occasion of

the celebration of your birth

Children are a blessing and
a gift from the LORD.

Psalm 127:3

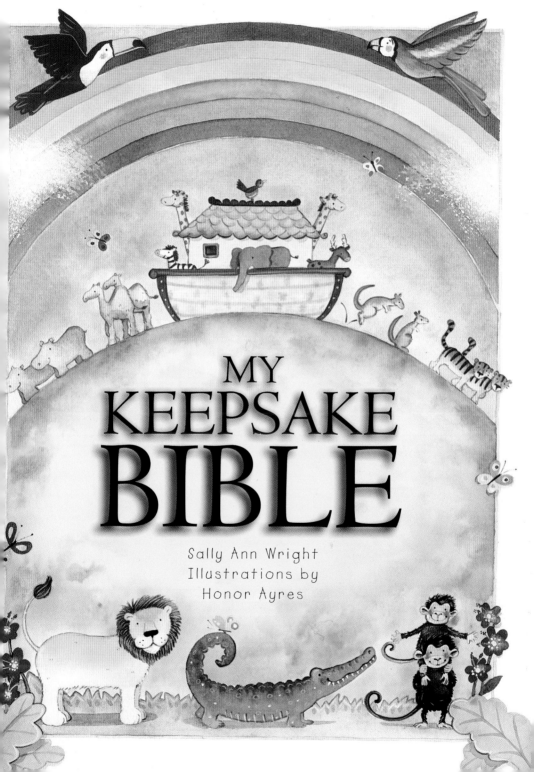

MY
KEEPSAKE
BIBLE

Sally Ann Wright
Illustrations by
Honor Ayres

Father God,
Creator of all that is good,
thank you for the gift
of this precious child
entrusted to our care.
Thank you for the miracle of new life
and the mystery
of human love.

This is me!

My name is

D'Angelo Lee Newkirk

I was born on

March 19, 2016

I was born at this address

New Hanover Regional Medical Center
2131 S. 17th Street, Wilmington, NC 28401

I weighed

6 lbs 4 oz

My eyes are

Brown

My hair is

Black

My home address is

304 Michigan Ave
Wilmington, NC 28401

My grandfather's name

Angelo Newkirk

Date and place of birth

| |

My grandmother's name

Ivy Gail Banks

Date and place of birth

| |

My father's name

Tony Andreus Newkirk

Date and place of birth

08/17/84   Wilmington, NC

This is my family

My grandfather's name

Norman Lee Kinsey

Date and place of birth

01/ /

My grandmother's name

Gloria M. Kinsey

Date and place of birth

12/27/   Wilmington, NC

My mother's name

Gloria Elaine Noble

Date and place of birth

1/2/89   Corpus Christi, Texas

My name

D'Angelo Lee Newkirk

Jesus, Friend of little children,
be a friend to me;
take my hand, and ever keep me
close to thee.

Walter J. Mathams

My Progress

I first smiled

....

I cut my first tooth

....

I first sat up

....

I first crawled

....

My first words

....

I first walked

....

My favorite things

Mommy, Daddy, and Big
Brother Kwentyn

CONTENTS
Bible Stories and Prayers

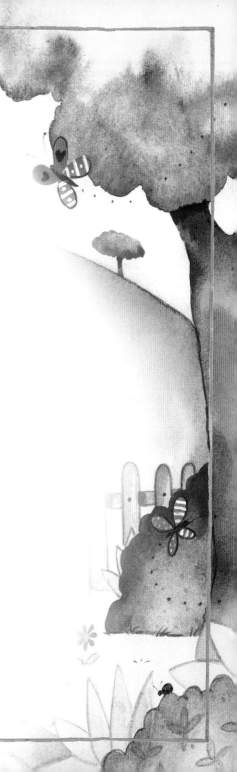

The Story of Creation

Long ago, at the very beginning, God was there. God made the first light shine in the darkness. He made high mountains surrounded by deep

14

water and rushing waterfalls.

God made the leafy trees and bright scented flowers; the sun, moon, and stars.

God made silvery fish and buzzing bees, song-birds and bright butterflies.

God made elephants and hippos, zebras, rhinos, and giraffes; cats, dogs, rabbits, and goldfish.

God made people to look after his beautiful world.

Everything in God's world was good.

Prayers

Thank you, God, for the world you have made.
For the warmth of the sun,
For the rain which makes things grow,
For the woods and the fields,
For the sea and the sky,
For flowers, trees, and animals,
For families, friends, and holidays,
For all your gifts,
Thank you, God.

16

Creator God, thank you for pets,
for the special friends we love to play with:
for furry cats and playful dogs,
for hamsters in wheels, and long-eared rabbits.
Help us always to remember to look after them well,
as part of the world you have made.

When Things Went Wrong

The first people were God's friends. Adam and Eve lived in a beautiful garden, and God gave them everything they needed.

"Eat anything you like," God said, "except from that tree over there."

But a wiggly serpent crept up to Eve one day.

"Did God really tell you not to eat from that tree?" he hissed. "Go on, try it—it looks juicy and sweet."

18

The fruit did look juicy and sweet. Eve took some and tasted it. Then Adam tasted it too.

Suddenly everything was different. Adam and Eve felt ashamed that they had done the only thing that God had told them not to do.

God's world was no longer good and perfect.

Noah's Ark

"Build an ark," said God to Noah. "Save your family and all the animals from the flood that will cover the earth."

Noah built the ark, a very, very big boat. All the animals came to Noah, two by two by two, and he kept them safe inside the ark.

Then the rain came, big, loud drops that soon became a stream. The stream became a river and the river became a sea of water that covered everything.

When the water went down, Noah, his family, and all the animals were free at last to start again. And God sent a beautiful rainbow.

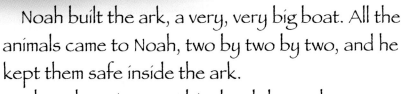

Prayers

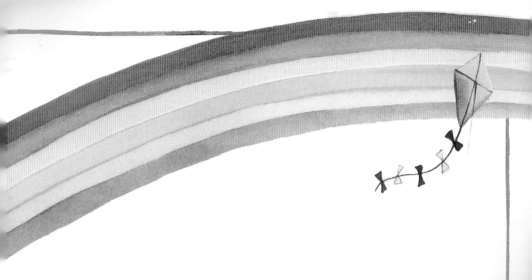

May the Lord bless us and watch over us.
May the Lord make his face shine upon us
and be gracious to us.
May the Lord look kindly on us
and give us peace;
and the blessing of God almighty,
the Father, the Son, and the Holy Spirit,
be with us and remain with us now and every day.

Based on Numbers 6

God Chooses Abraham

Abraham trusted God. So when God told him to move to a new home in a new country, Abraham took his wife, Sarah, and his nephew Lot and all his animals. They didn't know where they were going and they didn't know how long it would take them.

Abraham and Sarah had no children, but one starry night, God made them a promise.

"Come and look at the stars,"

24

God said. "One day there will
be as many people in your family
as there are stars in the sky."

Abraham knew that God always keeps
his promises. They waited a long time, but
they were very happy when baby Isaac was born.
It was the start of their very big family.

Isaac's Baby Boys

When Isaac was a man, Abraham wanted him to marry a girl who loved God too. He was very happy when Isaac married Rebekah.

They were all very happy when Rebekah gave birth to twins—two little baby boys and twice as much work!

The boys were very different. Esau had lots of red hair. Jacob had not much hair at all.

They grew up to be different too. Esau became a hunter, an outdoor man, and he was his father's favorite son. Jacob loved to cook. He was good company for his mother, and she loved him best.

Jacob Tricks His Father

Isaac grew to be an old man. He couldn't see very well at all. One day he asked Esau to go hunting so he could have his favorite meal in the evening.

"Then I will ask God to bless you when I am gone."

But Rebekah helped Jacob dress up in Esau's smelly clothes and put animal skins on his arms and neck so he felt hairy like his brother.

28

"You sound like Jacob . . . but you smell and feel like my son Esau," said Isaac. "May God bless you always and give you good things all your life. . . ."

Esau was very angry when he found that Jacob had taken his father's blessing from him!

Prayers

Thank you, Father God,
that you made me and I am special to you.
Thank you that you know all about me.
You know when I wake up
and when I go to sleep.
You know when I am at home
and when I go out.
You know when I am sad
and when I am happy.
You know when I am lonely
or when I have lots of friends.
You know when I am cross
or grumpy and do bad things
and when I am kind to other people.
Thank you that you know me
and you still love me, just as I am.

Based on Psalm 139

Joseph's Special Coat

God did bless
Jacob. He married
and had a huge
family! But like his
parents before
him, Jacob had a
favorite son.

Joseph knew that his
father loved him more than his
brothers. Sometimes it made him proud and
boastful. So when Jacob gave him a beautiful
coat, his brothers were very unhappy—so
unhappy that they began to plot to get rid
of him.

They waited for the right moment—and
sold him to some passing traders on their
way to Egypt. Joseph would be sold as a
slave. . . .

But the brothers told Jacob that his favorite son had been killed by a wild animal. Jacob thought he would never be happy again.

Good Things Come from Bad

Bad things happened to Joseph, but God was looking after him.

First Joseph worked hard for a kind master. Everything was fine until . . . someone told lies about him and he was sent to prison.

Joseph worked hard in prison. If he hadn't been in prison maybe he wouldn't have been asked to meet—the great king of Egypt himself!

Joseph worked hard for the king and became a Very Important Man in Egypt. He was so important that all his family came to live with him there. Jacob was very happy

to know that his dead son was alive after all.

So it was that Abraham's VERY big family went to live in Egypt for many, many years.

Miriam's Baby Brother

A long time after Joseph died, there was a big, bad king in Egypt. He was afraid because there were so many of Abraham's family living there.

First the king made them into slaves. Then he sent his soldiers to throw all their baby boys into the river!

Miriam watched her mother hide her baby brother in a basket by the river. Then Miriam watched over the basket to see what would happen.

After a while, a princess found the basket.

"You must belong to one of the slaves," she said. "I would like to keep you."

Big sister Miriam brought her mother to the princess to be his nurse. The soldiers couldn't hurt baby Moses now.

37

Prayers

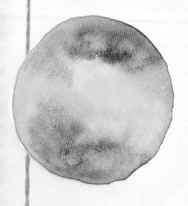

O Lord God, you are so great!
When I look at the sky,
and the moon and the stars,
I feel so tiny.
I don't understand why
you care about me.
Lord God, you are great,
but you are also kind and good.

Be here in the darkness, Lord;
watch over me and keep me safe this night.
Bless those who are far from home,
or sad, or lonely, or afraid,
and bring them light in their darkness,
your peace to help them,
and your love to comfort them.

Based on Psalm 8

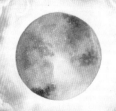

Frogs, Flies, and Buzzy Things

Moses grew up in the palace, but he saw that his people were badly treated. He hated it. One day he stopped a man beating a slave— but he killed the man instead. Then Moses ran away!

A very long time later, God told Moses it was time to go back to see the king.

"I want you to tell the king to let my people go!"

The king did not want to! They were his slaves! So 10 terrible plagues were seen in Egypt with frogs and flies and all sorts of horrible things invading the land until . . . the king told Moses to take the people and GO!

The Road to Freedom

God appeared as a tall cloud to
show his people the way to go every
day. God appeared as a tall fire to
show them the way to go every night.

When they reached the Red
Sea, Moses lifted his stick, and the
wind blew a path across the sea so
everyone could cross over safely on
dry land.

God's people were no longer
slaves in Egypt! They were free!

God provided food when the
people were hungry. God provided
water when they were thirsty.

43

Ten Rules for Life

God gave his people Ten Commandments. If they lived by these rules they would be happy with each other and live in peace.

"I am your God, the true and living God who made heaven and earth. Do not worship any other.

"Don't make anything else into a god and worship it.

"The name of God is special and holy. Use it when you pray, but do not use it as a swear word.

"Keep one day special so you can rest and have time to worship.

"Obey your father and mother.

"Life is precious. Don't murder anyone.

"Don't steal someone else's husband or wife.

"Don't steal anything!

"Don't tell lies about other people.

"Don't be jealous of things other people have."

Prayers

Lord Jesus,
you are the Good Shepherd.
You look after me and care for me.
Lord Jesus, Good Shepherd,
Look after my family and friends today.

Loving Father, please look after all
who are not well.
Comfort those who are in pain,
or who are worried or sad.
Give peace to those who are old
or frightened.
Help us to be loving
and helpful to our families,
kind to everyone we know,
and generous to anyone
who needs our help.

Gideon
Trusts God

Gideon was hiding. He was frightened by his neighbors, the fierce Midianites.

Things were not going well. God's people had promised to love God—but then they forgot all about their promises. So Gideon was very surprised to be visited by an angel.

"God has chosen you to help his people," said the angel.

"But I am not brave or clever," said Gideon. "Are you sure God wants me?"

God showed Gideon that he did. God made Gideon's woolly fleece wet when the ground was dry, and he made Gideon's woolly fleece dry when the ground was wet with dew!

Then Gideon trusted God and helped his people to make the Midianites go away so they could live in peace once more.

49

The Boy Who Listened

Samuel lived in God's Temple. He was learning about God and the right way to live.

One night Samuel woke to hear someone calling his name. He thought it was Eli, the priest.

"Here I am," said Samuel.

"I didn't call you," said Eli. "Go back to bed."

But Samuel heard the voice again.

"Here I am," said Samuel.

"I didn't call you," said Eli. "Go back to bed."

Then Samuel heard the voice again.

This time Eli knew it was God calling Samuel.

"Tell God you're listening to him," said Eli.

"I'm listening, God," said Samuel. "Speak to me."

Samuel always listened to God after that and helped to guide God's people.

The Big, Scary Giant

David was a shepherd boy, the youngest of eight brothers.

David watched the big, scary giant march up and down shouting with his big, scary voice, "Who will come and fight me?"

The big, scary giant was called Goliath. He wore big, scary armor and had a big, scary sword. He frightened the soldiers—he even frightened King Saul!

"I'll fight him," said David. "God has always helped me fight lions and bears when I looked after my sheep. He will help me now."

David whirled a pebble around in his sling. Then . . . *crash*! Goliath fell to the ground with a big, scary noise. Now he wouldn't frighten anyone again!

Prayers

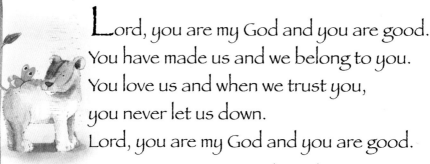

Lord, you are my God and you are good.
You have made us and we belong to you.
You love us and when we trust you,
you never let us down.
Lord, you are my God and you are good.

Based on Psalm 100

God, you are my hope and my strength,
always there in times of trouble;
therefore I will not be afraid,
even though things are difficult for me.

Based on Psalm 46

I love you, Lord,
because you heard me when I asked for help.
You listened when I needed you,
and you helped me because you love me.

Based on Psalm 116

A Very Special Gift

Solomon was very young when he became king.

"What gift would you like me to give you?" asked God.

Did Solomon want to be rich? Did he want to be famous? Did he want people to be afraid of him?

"I would like to be good and wise, fair and just and true," said Solomon. "I want to be a good king who rules his people well."

God was so pleased with Solomon's answer that he made Solomon good and wise, fair and just—but he also made him rich and famous.

People everywhere knew that God had blessed Solomon.

God Takes Care Of Elijah

It had stopped raining. The earth was dry and thirsty. The people were dry and thirsty. It was all because King Ahab had stopped talking to God.

God told Elijah where he could find a little stream with

cool, clear water. God sent large, black ravens to Elijah with food in their beaks. God took care of Elijah.

When the stream dried up, God sent Elijah to a kind woman who shared her last meal with him. But for as long as she shared with Elijah, God made sure that her little jar of flour and her little bottle of oil did not run out.

God took care of Elijah.

Fire and Rain

Elijah went back to King Ahab. It was time to choose.

"Our God is the living God," said Elijah. "Why are you worshiping a stone statue? It is time to choose who the real God is—and then worship him. Now, ask your pretend god to send down fire."

"Come on!" shouted the people who worshiped a stone statue. "Light our fire! Do something!"

Nothing happened.

Then it was Elijah's turn.

"Lord, let everyone see that you are the one true and living God," he prayed.

Fire fell from heaven and showed everyone that God was real. The people worshiped God.

Then God sent rain once more to the earth.

God Heals Naaman

Naaman had spots and sore places all over his skin. In his house was a little servant girl who wanted to help.

"Go to the prophet in my country," she said. "I know he will ask God to heal you."

So Naaman went to visit the prophet, Elisha.

"Go and wash in the river Jordan seven times," said Elisha's servant.

Elisha hadn't prayed for him—he had told him
to take a bath in a muddy river. Elisha hadn't even
come to see Naaman—he had sent a servant!

But Naaman bathed in the river seven times,
and the spots and sore places vanished. The
servant girl was right—God could heal him!

Prayers

Be kind to us and bless us, Lord.
Smile on us and give us your peace.
Let the whole world sing for joy
because you are wise and good.
Thank you for giving us all
that we need and for blessing us
day by day.

Based on Psalm 67

Please help me, Lord.
I know you can help me because
you are the God who made heaven and earth!
I know you will always take care of me.
You promise that you will watch over me,
day and night, wherever I am
and whatever I am doing.
Thank you, Lord!

Based on Psalm 121

Jonah and the Big Fish

The people who lived in Nineveh were
cruel and wicked. God told Jonah
to take them a message,
but Jonah didn't want to

go. Instead he ran away.
Jonah sailed away on a
ship, but he forgot that you
can't run away from God.
The wind howled and the
waves crashed. And Jonah
knew it was all his fault.
"Throw me into the sea!" said
Jonah. The sailors threw him
overboard . . . and watched as a
huge sea creature swallowed him whole.

Jonah sat inside the fish
and prayed.
  The big fish spat Jonah
out of its mouth onto dry
land, and Jonah took God's message
to Nineveh. The people were sorry for the
bad things they had done. They asked God to
forgive them and help them change their ways.
And God did!

Some Very Brave Men

Shadrach, Meshach, and Abednego lived far from their home, in Babylon. One day the king told everyone to bow down and worship a golden statue.

"There'll be trouble if you don't!" said a messenger. "You must worship that golden statue or be thrown into a fiery furnace!"

68

"We will only worship the one true God," they said. So the three men were thrown into the fiery furnace.

But God sent an angel to keep them safe. Shadrach, Meshach, and Abednego did not get burned at all. When the king brought them out of the fiery furnace, he knew that their God was the one true God who could save people.

Daniel and the Lions

Daniel was the king's friend. Daniel was also God's friend. Daniel loved God and prayed to him three times every day.

But Daniel was not the friend of the king's men. They didn't like Daniel at all.

"Let's make a new law," they told the king. "People must pray to you because you are great and powerful—or be thrown to the lions."

Daniel still loved God and prayed to him three times every day, just as he had before. So Daniel was thrown to the lions.

When the king went to the lions' den next
morning, he was very happy to find Daniel still
alive and well!

"Your God really IS great and powerful," said
the king.

71

Prayers

Let everyone know that you alone are God!
Let them praise you!
For you are great and do wonderful things.
Teach me to do what is right, Lord,
so that my life will be good
and I will do nothing to hurt anyone else.

Based on Psalm 86

I'll praise you, God,
and I'll worship you
because you are so wonderful,
and you made the whole wide world!
You're great and good,
marvelous and mighty,
ever loving, everlasting,
everywhere.

Mary and
the Angel

God thought Mary was very special. One day he sent the angel Gabriel to see her.

"Don't be afraid," said the angel. "God has sent me to tell you that you are going to have a baby. The baby will be God's own Son, and Jesus will be his name."

"But I am not even married yet. How can I have a baby?" said Mary.

"Don't worry, Mary," Gabriel said. "Nothing is impossible for God."

Mary was happy, even if she was a bit afraid. She told Joseph and he promised to take care of her and God's Son. And not long afterward, she found she was expecting a baby.

The Baby in the Manger

Mary gave birth to her baby son in Bethlehem. She went there with Joseph because the Roman Emperor wanted to count his people.

Mary made a bed for Jesus in the manger, because there was no room at the inn.

That night, angels appeared in the sky, bringing the good news of Jesus' birth to some shepherds who were looking after their sheep.

The shepherds ran to Bethlehem to look for the baby. They found him with Mary and Joseph and told them all about the message of the angels. Then they told everyone they saw what had happened that night.

Prayers

Lord Jesus,
you were a tiny baby
in a manger, in Bethlehem.
You grew up to be a man
who helped people who were ill,
or sad, or lonely,
and you showed us how to love
other people as God does.
Thank you, Lord Jesus.

A long time ago,
Mary put her baby in a manger.
Thank you, God, that today we can know him.
A long time ago,
the angels sang because Jesus was born.
Thank you, God, that today we can worship him.
A long time ago,
shepherds hurried to see their Savior.
Thank you, God, that today we can serve him.
A long time ago,
wise men brought gifts to Jesus.
Thank you, God, that today we can love him.

May the joy of the angels,
the wonder of the shepherds,
and the peace of Jesus Christ
fill our hearts this Christmastime.

John
Baptizes
Jesus

Jesus was a good
little boy. Then he
grew up to be a good man.

One day he went to see
John, who was baptizing people in the
river Jordan.

"Come and tell God you are sorry," said
John to all the people. "Tell him you want to
do good things. Show him you are sorry by
coming to be baptized."

"Baptize me," said Jesus.

80

"But you don't
need to be baptized,"
said John. "You have done
no bad things!"
"Please, I want to do this," said Jesus.
So John baptized him.
Then they heard God's voice from heaven.
"This is my Son. I love him."

Jesus and His Friends

"Come with me," Jesus said to Peter and Andrew.

"Come with me," he said to James and John.

"Leave your fishing nets and help me tell people how good God is. Help me to make bad people good and sad people happy. Help me heal people who are blind or deaf or cannot walk."

"Come with me," Jesus called to Matthew the tax collector.

Twelve men left what they were doing and decided to be special friends, people who went wherever Jesus was. They were Peter, Andrew, James, John, Philip, Bartholomew, Matthew, Thomas, another James, Thaddeus, Simon, and Judas.

God Loves You

"God loves you," Jesus told everyone. "Don't worry too much about food and drink and clothes. Be like the birds in the sky and the

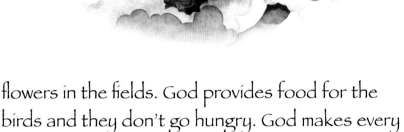

flowers in the fields. God provides food for the birds and they don't go hungry. God makes every flower beautiful!

"Trust God—he will give you what you need. Love God—and share what you have with each other."

"God cares about the tiniest sparrow," said Jesus. "And you are much more important to God than the sparrow. God knows you and he cares about you. God will keep you safe in his strong, kind hands."

Prayers

Our Father in heaven,
hallowed be your name.
Your kingdom come,
your will be done,
on earth as in heaven.
Give us today our daily bread.
Forgive us our sins,
as we forgive those who sin against us.
Lead us not into temptation,
but deliver us from evil.
For the kingdom,
the power, and the glory are yours,
now and for ever.

Based on Matthew 6

The Hole in the Roof

"Excuse me!"

"Careful now!"

Lifting their friend carefully through all the people and then up the steps beside the house was not easy. But the four men wanted their friend to meet Jesus. They wanted Jesus to meet their friend—and help him to walk again!

The crowd was a problem. So they planned to make a hole in the roof and lower him down into the room below where Jesus was talking to a crowd of people.

The plan worked.

Jesus knew what they wanted. And Jesus made their friend well again so that he could pick himself up and walk home! People could hardly believe what had happened in that room that day.

Jesus Calms a Storm

Soon people were
coming from everywhere
to ask Jesus to heal
them or heal people they
knew. Now Jesus was
tired.

Jesus and his friends
sailed across Lake
Galilee. Soon Jesus fell
asleep to the sound of
the gentle waves.

The storm came
suddenly, with a howling
wind and claps of thunder, with
whooshing waves that rocked the
boat up and down, up and down.

"Wake up!" the men shouted. "Help
us or we will drown!"

Jesus stood up and told the wind
to drop. Jesus told the waves to stop.

And everything was calm again.
Jesus' friends were no longer
afraid of the storm; but they
wondered just who Jesus was.

Jesus Heals a Little Girl

"Please come quickly!" Jairus was almost pulling Jesus through the crowd of people. "My little girl is very ill."

Jesus went with Jairus. But there were many people there wanting Jesus to help them.

"It's too late!" a man shouted to Jairus. "I'm so sorry—but your little girl has died."

Jesus spoke gently to Jairus. "Trust me," Jesus said. "It will be okay."

They went into Jairus's house, and Jesus took the little girl's hand.

"Wake up, little girl," Jesus said.

Jairus's daughter opened her eyes and smiled at Jesus.

"I think she would like something to eat," said Jesus, smiling at her happy parents.

The Little Boy's Picnic

There were thousands of people out on the hillside. And they were hungry.

They had been listening to Jesus tell stories about how much God loved them. Jesus had also healed people who were blind or deaf or hurting. Jesus was so kind and good they could be with him all day.

"Would you like to share my lunch?" a little boy asked Jesus. He offered five pieces of bread and two little fish.

"Yes, please," said Jesus. Then he thanked God.

The disciples shared the picnic with all the people there—ALL the people there! And somehow everyone had enough to eat, and no one was hungry. It was a miracle.

Prayers

O God, your generous love
surrounds us,
and everything we enjoy
comes from you.

Yours, Lord, are the greatness, the power,
the glory, and the majesty,
for everything we have comes from you.

Based on 1 Chronicles 29:11

All good gifts around us
Are sent from heaven above.
Then thank the Lord, O thank the Lord,
For all his love.

For every cup and plateful,
Lord, make us truly grateful.

The Good Samaritan

"God wants you to love him and to be kind to other people—even if they are strangers," said Jesus.

"Listen: a man was attacked and robbed while walking on a lonely road. The man hurt all over.

"He heard footsteps and thought someone was coming to help him. But the footsteps went away. Later he heard more footsteps . . . but they went away too.

"Then the man heard the sound of a donkey coming closer. *Clip, clop, clip, clop.* The man with

the donkey came from another country. But his footsteps did not go away. The man bathed his wounds and helped him onto the donkey. He paid for an innkeeper to look after him till he was well.

"Be kind to people, like the Good Samaritan," said Jesus.

The Loving Father

"God is like a good father who loves his children," said Jesus.

"God is like the man who owned a hundred sheep. When only one went missing, he made sure the ninety-nine sheep were safe before he looked everywhere for the missing sheep.

"He climbed steep hills and looked in prickly bushes. He didn't rest until he heard the faint cry of his lost sheep. Then he brought it home on his shoulders, happy that he had found the one sheep that was lost."

Prayers

Lord Jesus,
the wind and the waves obey you.
Deaf people hear because of you.
Blind people see because of you.
Lame people walk because of you.
Dead people live because of you.
Help me to obey you,
to hear you, to see you in those around me,
to walk where you want me to be,
to live my life serving you by helping others.

Lord, make us instruments of your peace.
Where there is hatred, let us sow love;
Where there is injury, let there be pardon;
Where there is discord, union;
Where there is doubt, faith;
Where there is despair, hope;
Where there is darkness, light;
Where there is sadness, joy;
For your mercy and for your truth's sake.

St. Francis of Assisi

The Man Who Said Thank You

One day Jesus saw ten men standing in a huddle, hiding their faces. They were afraid to come near. They were afraid to be seen.

Jesus knew they suffered from leprosy, a bad skin disease that made their lives miserable.

"Go back to your homes," said Jesus. "Be well—God has healed you."

It was a miracle! Nine

of the men went home,
happy that they were well
again. One man came to
speak to Jesus.

"Thank you!" the man
said. "Thank you for
healing me."

Jesus smiled kindly
at the man. But he
wondered why no one
else had said thank you.

105

The Blind Beggar

There was a blind man in Jericho who sat asking for money as people walked by. He wished he could see so he could work like other people.

One day he heard a huge crowd of people coming along. He shook his begging bowl. But

then he heard the name of Jesus.

"Jesus!" he called out. "Over here!"

The blind man knew who Jesus was. He knew that Jesus could heal him.

"What can I do for you?" asked Jesus.

"Please—I just want to see!" the man said.

So Jesus healed him—and the man was so happy, he started following Jesus along the road.

The Man Who Climbed a Tree

Zacchaeus was up a tree.

He had wanted to see Jesus so much. Zacchaeus didn't have any friends because he worked for the Romans. And because, if he was honest with himself, he had cheated lots of people out of their money. Three coins for the Romans and one for Zacchaeus.

But now Jesus seemed to be looking right at him.

"Come down," said Jesus. "I'd like to come to your house today."

Zacchaeus couldn't stop the smile going from ear to ear. Not long afterward, Zacchaeus knew that Jesus was his friend—and he started to share his money with the poor and repay the people he had cheated.

"That's why I'm here," said Jesus.

Riding on a Donkey

Crowds of people were making their way into Jerusalem. Jesus and his friends were among them, all going for the Passover Festival.

But Jesus was not on foot this time. He had asked his friends to find him a young donkey to ride, and there he was, on the donkey's back, trotting slowly through the gates of the city.

"Look! Here comes Jesus!" someone shouted.

Suddenly people started to wave and cheer. Others waved palm branches.

"Hooray for Jesus! Jesus is our king!"

Lots of them knew about the good things

Jesus had done. They loved him.

But not everyone was so happy. Some men stood to one side, frowning and plotting.

Look After Each Other

Later in the week, Jesus and his friends met to eat together. But instead of sitting down with them, Jesus knelt and washed the dust from their feet. He dried them gently with a towel.

Peter was shocked. Surely this was a servant's job!

"Let me do this, Peter," said Jesus. "If I can do this for you, perhaps you will also do it for each other. No one is too important to look after someone else. This is how people will know that you are my friends. Take care of each other. Love one another in this way."

Prayers

Lord Jesus,
you told us not to be worried about anything,
but I am worried about tomorrow.
Help me not to be afraid
and to trust you to help me.

Based on Matthew 6

God be in my head, and in my understanding;
God be in my eyes, and in my looking;
God be in my mouth, and in my speaking;
God be in my heart, and in my thinking;
God be at my end, and at my departing.

Sarum Primer

Be near me, Lord,
in the dark moments of my life.
Help me when I feel so sad
that I cannot remember
what it feels like to be happy.

I need you, Lord.
Please come close to me.
Help me, rescue me, protect me.

Based on Psalm 69

115

The Last Supper

Jesus gave some food to Judas. He knew that the man who had once been his friend had taken 30 silver coins to betray him to the religious leaders.

"Not all of you here are my friends," Jesus said, looking at Judas.

"I would do anything for you, Lord," Peter said, "even die for you!"

"Peter, before the rooster crows, you will say three times that you don't even know me," said Jesus sadly.

Jesus shared the bread with them. "This is my body, broken for you," he said. He shared a cup of wine. "This is my blood, spilled for you."

Jesus Prays in the Garden

After supper, Jesus took his friends to a garden
of olive trees. He asked them to keep watch while
he prayed.

"I will do anything you ask of me, Father God,"

said Jesus. "But please, help me to be brave."

When Jesus went back to his friends, he found they had fallen asleep while he was praying. Jesus felt sad and lonely.

Jesus woke them, but already there were the sounds of people coming through the trees. There were torches and flares in the darkness. Judas greeted Jesus with a kiss, so the soldiers knew which man they should arrest and march away.

Crosses on a Hillside

The friends had run away. Only Peter and John had followed to find out what was happening to Jesus. But Peter was afraid—and told people he didn't even know Jesus—three times!

Jesus was questioned. They knew he had done nothing wrong. But his enemies, the teachers and leaders, wanted him out of the way.

Jesus, the man who had healed people, helped

them, and been kind to them, was crucified on a hillside between two thieves.

Jesus asked God to forgive the soldiers who hurt him and everyone in the world for everything they'd ever done wrong. Jesus was dying for them.

Jesus took his last breath and died.

Where Is Jesus?

Jesus was buried in a cave on Friday evening, and a big, heavy stone was rolled in front of it.

Early on Sunday morning, the women went there—but found that the big, heavy stone had been rolled away—and the cave was empty!

"Jesus isn't here," said an angel. "Go and tell everyone—he is alive again!"

Some of the women ran to tell the others, but Mary Magdalene stayed by the empty cave, crying. She could not understand what had happened until she heard a kind voice behind her.

"Mary," he said.

Mary knew that voice. It was Jesus! Jesus was alive and Mary had seen him!

Thomas Meets Jesus

Jesus went to see his friends when they were together behind locked doors. He shared a meal with them. But Thomas had not been there.

"I can't believe it," said Thomas. "I won't believe he is alive unless I see Jesus myself."

"But it's true," said his friends. "We've seen him. We've spoken to him."

A week later, Jesus came again. This time Thomas was there.

"Hello, Thomas," said Jesus. "Look at me. Touch the wounds in my hands. Now do you believe that it's me—and I'm alive?"

"Jesus!" gasped Thomas. "It really is you!"

Friends Meet Jesus

Peter and his friends hadn't seen Jesus for a few days.

"I'm going fishing," said Peter one night.

Six of his friends went too. They fished all night, but they didn't catch any fish at all, not one. At sunrise, they heard a man's voice from the shore.

"Have you caught anything?" he called.

"Nothing," they shouted back.

"Put out your net on the other side," said the man. Then the net was full to bursting with slippery, silvery fish.

"It's Jesus!" Peter said, jumping into the water.

Then all the friends had a barbecued breakfast with Jesus.

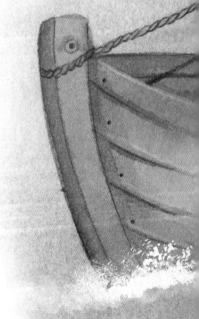

Prayers

Lord, comfort and heal all those who suffer.
Give courage to those who are afraid.
Comfort those who have no hope,
and give joy to all who are sad.

Thank you, Lord Jesus,
that the sadness of your cruel death
on Good Friday has a happy ending.
Thank you, Lord Jesus,
that you rose from the dead
so that one day I can live
with you in heaven.

Go and Tell Everyone!

God sent the Holy Spirit to help Peter and John and his other friends. They weren't frightened anymore. They were bold and brave.

"Jesus is God's Son," Peter said to huge crowds of people. "He died on a cross because he loves you. Stop doing bad things. Tell Jesus you are sorry and he will forgive you."

A lot of people decided to trust God after listening to Peter. They prayed and had meals together. They shared together and took care of each other—just as Jesus had taught them.

They knew that God was always there to help them.

Share and Be Kind

Now there were not just a few people who loved Jesus and believed he was alive—there were thousands of them.

They helped each other and shared what they had with people who had little or nothing. God helped them to heal people who were ill or could not walk, just as Jesus had done.

People around them started to notice what was happening. Many were amazed and started to believe too. But some of the religious leaders were unhappy about the new Christians, as they were called, just as they had been unhappy about Jesus.

Saul Meets Jesus

Saul was one of the people who
loved God but thought the
Christians were wrong about
Jesus. He helped to find them and
make sure they went to prison.
Some of them were killed, too.

Saul was on the way to Damascus when
something amazing happened. Saul met Jesus.
First he saw a light so bright that it blinded him.
Then as he fell to the ground, Saul heard a voice.

"When you hurt my friends, you hurt me, too," said Jesus.

Now Saul knew for himself that Jesus was God's Son. It was not just a story—it was

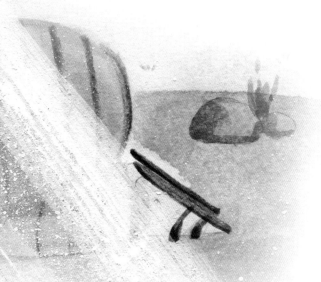

true! Saul wanted Jesus to be his friend too.

Now he was known by a new name. Saul became known as Paul.

Paul Is Shipwrecked!

Paul began to tell people everywhere that God loved them, and soon people in many places were baptized.

Paul and his friends made journeys to many places to tell people about Jesus. But sometimes their journeys were dangerous, and often Paul was put in prison. When Paul sailed to Rome, a terrible storm wrecked the ship. But God made sure everyone on board made it to the island of Malta.

Paul told people about Jesus in Malta, and later he did the same in Rome. Wherever he was, Paul shared the news about Jesus.

Paul's Thank-You Letters

While Paul was in Rome, far from his new Christian friends, he wrote lots of letters to them.

He wrote to thank them because they were praying for him, and he told them that he was asking God to look after them, too.

Paul reminded them to live as God wanted

them to—to be kind and forgiving to each other and to share what they had with others. He told them that the most important thing they could do was to love God. Then they would begin to act like him, loving other people too.

Prayers

May the peace of God,
which passes all understanding,
keep your heart and mind
in the knowledge and love of God,
and of his Son, Jesus Christ;
and the blessing of God almighty,
the Father, the Son, and the Holy Spirit,
be with you and remain with you always.

Based on Philippians 4

Now I lay me down to sleep,
I pray the Lord my soul to keep:
may God guard me through the night
and wake me with the morning light.

First U.S. edition by Tyndale House Publishers, Inc., 2015.

Visit Tyndale's website for kids at www.tyndale.com/kids.

TYNDALE and Tyndale's quill logo are registered trademarks of
Tyndale House Publishers, Inc.

The Tyndale Kids logo is a trademark of
Tyndale House Publishers, Inc.

My Keepsake Bible

For manufacturing information regarding this product,
please call 1-800-323-9400.

ISBN 978-1-4143-9867-9

Printed in China

20   19   18   17   16   15
 6   5   4   3   2   1